W0038310

MERCURIAL

OR IS THAT LIBERTY?

RACHELLE RAHMÉ

Fonograf Editions
Portland, OR

First Edition, First Printing

FONO41

Published by Fonograf Editions
www.fonografeditions.com

For information about permission to reuse any material from this
book, please contact Fonograf Ed. at info@fonografeditions.com.

Distributed by NYU Press
NYUPress.org

[c|mp]

Fonograf Editions is a proud member of the Community
of Literary Magazines and Presses

ISBN: 978-1-964499-57-4
ISBN (ebook): 978-1-964499-59-8
LCCN: 2024952689

MERCURIAL

OR IS THAT LIBERTY?

FONOGRAF EDITIONS

CONTENTS

From the mouth of the canon it snows.

RENÉ CHAR

Demos Demeanor

Semblance has carried its
        flag too long, its
right to build upon my sand.
I possess
        an immovable impregnance,
and now here comes a wave —
This wave and I belong together
        because I am built at
        its edges, and here I am
        stationed for sacrifice, you
        know, not to disappear,
        I will only be unmade,
        like the ancestor who
        scatters nothing, eats ash,
        a mushroom that hates
        salt, its intelligence
        beyond self-sacrifice.
A wave with no shoreline
        is let it be. Its extraterrestrial
        master with an ancient lever
I am composed, swallowed, swimming
and no longer semblance. A private
memory, hello pretty,
you without paradox, I insist,
gather up these grains, remake
this I, errant pile, patched with pits
and flakes of another, you decide

the going rate for correctness
                and the careen,
points clinging on gentle
                        fathomlessness.

Feeling Over Diction

I as all the different
   questions, as one of
   those knowing knots
     men's shoes
     the positive father
     where I can father an
understandable displacement
for soldiers to return to
   knot by knot.

Trouble with thinking is
you don't always have to.
Patience in the
   stomach is
vigilance in the shoulders.

Trouble with not-thinking,
   blanking, is
these other things think,
crawl, hide under
feeling over diction.

I ate an orange, read a
   book, I called
 you, something of it tasted
of barnyard when it
   cooled.

Better than music when a year ago jots when.

Moderation, asking each of the
        core to speak
a spell that
I sweat and
        keeps
on giving.

Skin shores,
luxury is something I
        borrow from the bourgeoisie,
their fingers long and slim on television,
poking at love in a trance
knowing how to forget
        from blank to blank
was a quiet
'I cannot live without you'
        playing yesterday.

Cueing

I don't get the hype, the trees are still
        green (though cueing),
the jig, embarrassment suites them, and
        the public feels okay about it.
The two have flowered, shame spears,
someone said take her by the ankles
        and pull
the wheel — torture first,
running as she is — why does the blood
        start at the point of running?
So I am never still, and
as she, I turn
am stretched to the membrane to
        be permeable and passed through
by cinematic cuts as
false engines to behold — the whole
        montage does not account for the
consciousness it depends on.

Pulsion

When I say ideal that
means what I want —

all the amenities of a plush sensitivity
with the limits between bodies that
          all bodily fluids face.

Why anyone would want to be
          a parent, I still don't know.
I'd be more interested in one
          upping your nihilism.
Foggy days in pursuit of
          no distraction,
carrot without question,
I follow both, I am late,
always late, it's so difficult to
          be contemporary.

Should we assume the
          poem does the idea
                    justice;
does the book do the
          painting justice?
The bed becomes a boat,
various platforms
virtual and otherwise resistant
          to experience,
the real ice.

Not a religious man, executed
        for the third time now,
        he turned red
for your ideal other
apart from
the goal.

Symbols unclear to me,
good and difficult to
        be a creature without work
        to do, thinking.

I am not particularly staunch
        independence,
have not a present
connection between a
        then and
now domestic sacred
heart in Sexton's chalice.

Ritual liturgical language
would eclipse
the mind's logic.

How deep down to build,
how far the soul is,
different life is, from death,
'oh for a' wanting
distance
buried under spotlight

to read this poem and
        bring her back
engaging in a shift of sorts
        that resurrects her
and acknowledges her
        finitude, acknowledges
life by circumscribing death

under the light, get under.

Shouting About Alien Love

Putting out an invitation,

something about _____
        that makes me act
        out of fear we're dying.
I dream of the yellowing
        no-hope book
till I can only
no longer lower
my anchor.
        Where I do sit among
        the newly tarred roofs
whose non-holes will keep
        our trinkets
from taking over and
        leaping up, evolution;
or is it just another battered
        sublation
one kiss to another
the strictness of our parents in
        youth to their childlike
old age
        the scattered seed?

Emerson Like Scripture

— "Adequate expression is rare."

To feel complete like an essay in
          your mouth escaping
is like my
breath drifting out there
          into the atmosphere
in smoke, legs shaking for need
of exercise and
          preferring study.

I spoke with you often to
          give the 'worldly' body
more iconic storms. Sitting up just-so
with apparatus to blame
and sparingly on
wet cement, cigarette filters,
          yellow discs, stars
spilling milk confessions at
          your service.

Missing persons remembered, Freddie
is walking alone in
          this early eventide,
wearing that blue suit that he wore to his
          nephew's funeral, rarely seen,
shaken by memory and that black hole when
          I cross you.

Even among plants, some thrive by
            indirect light
in my neighborhood, and I confess my outlook
is very off to you; so tell me
warmer, almost hot
            operative that gets us closer
to the multiple.

Offsets and ons, skeptical muse,
likes me to apply all experiences and
            others to this metric, inspired,
knows I will fail to consume thyself
            and will
                crawl again, a child.

After the Movie

That we dissolved in Mallorca;
you agreed you'd been pretty miserable
yourself, we'd take some time apart,
you went with John W (far apart)
to a movie; I for some thinking. I'd wanted
to go, but didn't, didn't say anything, I
was
       met by an ungodly creature
with travel pointers.
I was introduced to a famous pairing,
      writer/director, who said
if I wasn't right,
if I wanted to stay in Mallorca,
I could stay in his building where
only artists stay for
$135 a month. Parting, it
      wasn't right,
but it was a new now realizing
the border had been drawn.
      I troubled
the trolley/bus searching
      the city. I had
a problem of ends, I
couldn't buy a ticket, and the train
was due, and I didn't know
the laws for stowaways.
I sent a poem to
      the impossibly deployed.

I was offered a train of
            misgivings. I wrote
theses as marginalia, eyes
bloodshot, and was it facile?
            But I
don't want to sleep, I want
to walk. There's nowhere
            to go, I go round,
but it is only frontways immersive
and inconsistent in that.

To take care of the poem,
this is a life's profession,
            opportunity,
a living poet, rare.
If the lines aren't evidence
            enough,
she pushes herself a page,
and suicide is more noble
than accident
when it comes
            to windows.

But Camus died in a car wreck,
so did Pollack, so did Dean
            and we love our cars,
how and why we love them.

Ethics to limit suffering,
            when you hear me.

I know we are human
that is recognizable, that it
        can attest to our
own striving. How did we
know these words before
        the lexicon,
a legal term for exclusion,
        two ways. I have
one foot in, one out. Warm
bodies without
        all the jiggly stuff,
something mired in
history is under its possession.

How did your mother die?
In a room.
We were watching TV when her last
        free breaths fanned out,
a thimbleful.

All the woes that you
        hear me, the given
aspect of what will be done.
When I'm pushed out
        with my dreams
        at my ankles,
out of my hands, when
        it is said and suffices,
deep abiding poem that
        is composed in bits
I can exchange and digest.

Deep Abiding Poem that Is Composed
of Bits I can Exchange and Digest

I dreamt of a hall of dark corners
        above the haunted
two stanza poem — what
dreams of being street bound
        in England could
        do to me

It's like being on hunger beach,
seashells and sandwiches
_____'s
books
reading
writing
reason
responsibility

Hieroglyphics Then and Now

The bluejay is lost
        cry and listen for cries
cry into the wind to have
the one cry return
dispassion
things I do for others
things I do for myself
things I do compulsively
things I was taught
things I don't know
things I've seen
things I've done
        on the train

One last line
        one last word
        on poetry

Rarely do they come together
rarely do they agree
though that was already the source of
the deal you may no longer want
yet now pursue
        and offer
        in elegant clarity.

Ultraviolet Increment

I collide with monoliths
       in verse
wave of closures across time
to alter your
turret hiding between
       seasons.

Return to the room
flung in Pollack
       gestures
splatter jeans
burn bright
on the body wrapped for
       an unapologetic art.

Rehearse my work on Janus
it just takes a linoleum floor
       and low ceiling
for ardor, that the other
inference,
       to cover an afternoon
diversion with form.

Wave of closures
divisible expenditure
as if you weren't in motion
and couldn't tell the extent

to which
        her forgoing ritual,
so obvious, was
trying to score.

Double Procession

When my poem is in my
        blood, so you, too, course
and may at least remind me
of something unknown
        to date,
a pause in the daylong abyss,
I repass over again,
        undoes me.

'Do as I do, not as I say' may
        be equally perplexing, but is
        it more in practice? — and
        then we learn to speak
        differently, where
you never changed, and now
        there is no measure.

Undoes the day's bandage
in shedding dress
        — attends to our difference
        to reappear
to a room, and it is usually
in mute colors,
        where I am at and why.

Mercurial, or Is That Liberty?

They are setting up
        through elocution
a prisoner's checks and
light sleeps
in tactical effect so holes
        and their daylight
leak energy.

Their logic
becomes so precise it is an atom's
        width, it
stretches along ex nihilo,
finely stretches
        across a twin fissure.

Of a monstrous
        vast chroma and sign,
of a living and finite
        object,
the self, utility art cult,
        single natural obsession,
a person
        devoted to   controversial
        disputation
deified in the art and practice of
        polemics.

Platform Briars

Frank is downstairs
      talking about   "that
was a pretty girl that just passed."
I can't see her, I try, but I can
      see him looking after
her, happy in hopes that she'll
      turn.

Change of scenery on a
      day so reflective of change.

To consider the well-known painter
in the room
      and the model who
set the lights up to
illuminate the
      platform briars.

Seasons spare the wild sun,
heat decreates
      mewl by mewl,
Frank, Frank's daughter, her
friend, prop church roses on
generations in a vacuum with
little sense of humility. Why a
      conversation at the point of
seeming dated, becomes off
then speechless,
      but always in the new.

What the Rich Eat

The difference between reading to conjure and
reading to experience disquiet
                                    seems rich.

Only the rich have things
              that come to them at midnight.
For the rest, it's between restless sleep
and likes to laugh.

              The laughing
is crying really —
              had other things to do, birthday babies,
              everything is confused, actually so
              simple, we need
to feed vision, says the prophetic nothing,
              gentle clap
of technology's finest innocent.

I'm on Montauk having a beer with Jim and Andy.
I bear them of course, but
oral history always ends in tears.

Sometimes it was fun, sometimes games,
one standing
              in a window
the other down below, listening for
              the cul-de-sac ring.

Rae says the plants grow like jazz —
when I don't
            know what I've planted and it
            keeps surprising me with fruit,
and I always find myself
            grazing on so
little to naught for money,
            only seems right
as the rock dove's ombre
tending to the black
black sheep of my black Jesus
            who is trying to tell you he is
complicated and holy, who is
            trying to explain
you'll have to
            visit me by degrees.

Approbation

What are we having tonight?
I couldn't respond because I didn't know
I have nothing to lose but a remote possibility
We're glad
I for one know we've had our ups and downs
We'll take
And to drink
I'd just stay in bed all day otherwise, we need a
    motivating factor
That's why we need to discuss what we're going to do
What are we having tonight?
We need to divide things in equal parts
I made a pre-investment
That's why we need to discuss what we're going to do
We're uh… well, I'm having
And I'm going to have
Can we have
Certainly
Are we ready to order?
I'll have
I'll have
I'll have the same
I'll have
I'll have
And we'll have
We'll have one of everything
We'll take

All but the Living

The town is the weather, no?
The town and the weather do not agree
        on the season.
There is both the there and the neither
for you to contend with until there is
        nothing above
        the humming threshold.

Certain animal companions know more
languages
        than you do,
they're studying
        while the figurative Rome
        takes its cold plunge.

I'll tell you all about the things I've managed
        to avoid
like when we found a parking space
        and the sewer caps whispered,
I can derive anything from a blue cap, where
        I would,
with the lid, constitute what I am not,
        obtain through risk ("brick
        laying") a solemn city.

Good Sex Under Capitalism Does Not Exist

A Polemic in Two Parts

I.

He wasn't white, he was Albanian,
and that stupid straight girl sitting on my lap.
As a red light called us, she said feminism.
String lights swing.
We know burning rubber, something that's not supposed
    to be burned.
You find moments in the day, a fuck boy bar.
When the gas prices go down, I'll do a cross country,
it costs me a buck fifty alone to drive around the city.
I absolutely hear it. We should go to Beacon *now*,
that's what we should do.
It was my idea to go
to Beacon,
and go down to the Tenderloin, be gay.
It's pretty there.

•

Banned from *Pumps*.
What do you have to do to get banned from that
place,
my god,
there was not a goddamn soul there.
I almost wish I were that focused.

•

If anyone is radical, she is the epitome.
Just let me go study,
leave me to
my nothings.

•

That I do fear I have evaded meaning
and someone's fire, my art without
technics.

What is good music for a suffering soul?
Art Ensemble of Chicago,
The Paris Session.
What's more song for a soul that's in pain?
Mortika,
Recordings from a Greek Underworld;
Lennie Tristano,
Descent into the Maelstrom.

•

It was picturesque and delicious
of you.

The next thing I know I am buying coke with him at 2am
under a bridge,
fucking,

I was thinking
this is not sustainable.

I can't achieve that level of creepiness.
I'm not in it for the long game.
Thursday through Saturday
it's literally brandishing
the head of your enemy
on television,
protected by my
corporate core,
a serial property collector,
and breeze to read,
as I like sportswriting but disdain sports,
fun fact, rainbow fish,
animals crawl into it, and it
gets bigger, and she
was a nun, why you remain
sweet, milky, smiling.

•

The cross situation,
where we meet in the body.

•

Now that we found love what are we going to
do with it.

•

A monarch way station,
certified fluttering, as you pass through vision.

•

The cross situation between your legs.

•

I know you're trying to
save me
for last;
it's the walk that's talking.

•

I know how you feel, wimp.
I'll miss this place, too,
the statue's penis, I wonder
if she'll notice; she'll notice.
It was just three days,
unlucky in love,
but supernatural in other affairs
like a stray.
So I loosen up.
Liberty or death.
I feel I don't know you, when you're
like this, thirsty,
a whole field of religious studies
gestured to in a wave.

8 bad years, that's all.
I know it's insane
to find a really good
book and read it all day,
without the need to communicate
the way your hair feels on ketamine.
I pretend
to want more,
your aspirations,
a blue, tepid spring,
tattoo of a gnat on your ass
for swatting.

II.

Good Sex Until Capitalism Does Not Exist

This night is comforting,
thanks for letting me in.
Okay to relax, no harm done.
Your life has nothing to do with convention,
the outside world has no meaning. Relax,
make friends with a being that you may
have seen before. We are all friends,
why would we not be? Nice to
meet new people, it puts trust
in those you know.
Then again, I'm nobody's buddy,
though I made peace with you,
as I'm in love with this place, the detritus,

and friends waiting
to cultivate a fading angel's smile.
Sometimes dressed in blindness,
the moon, sometimes made to explain
new strings. Why I am here.
Asylum is one of those
something-nothings.
I have all, am left
in soft questions, is there time to explain,
my dear friend Alice, that I changed
the word
from revolution to revolt
so as not to leave you lonely.
Though I heard that Marxists have
good sex, though I don't think they'd qualify
it with a moral good, not that binary,
it's that they do it a lot, so of course it gets better.
Where I'll stop you, gone,
you already hate this poem. Would you give
up good sex for revolution;
it's time for revolution and loneliness.
Might be there, too.
Simultaneous orbits, goings-round,
a cycle that is a situation of change,
I succumb to the muse,
abstract x-ray,
a painting or wound that
heads turn to see.
It times out, guitar part,
my story goes on, loses itself on you,

illusion of endless supply and alternate titles
is half full, though barely,
till you take a sip with your eye,
as you are thirsty and saving your last dollar.

Models for Peace

How quickly it burned up
and was gone, in the manner
they imagined they'd
once crashed landed on
this planet. Year one
burned up, and year two
was the after burn. No
chance in reversing its
dispersal, its definitive usage
burning, because
the atmosphere is always
incident to compression,
changing amplifications to
hear your innards whimper,
where you get really
beautiful in summer, 1508
E. Helen Ave., bootlegs
or bust, and find the wailing
words hiding somewhere.
Taking leaps at certain platitudes
and also feeling shy, which
means put out by myself,
as the white dress in
my dream makes fronds of them.
Resistance to any action
at all, projects taking
over life, I connect them
to my subconscious, which

I know by only three methods:
art production, bibliomancy,
intimacy, all involving very specific
acts just for their practice;
brainstorming, as it relates
to problem-solving, not shopping,
not driving. How close is too
close? How many degrees
of separation are adequate for
a lasting, making of a substantial
drab in that model-making
thing that breaks up a year.
Fall away, dash it to pieces,
always on display,
can't keep track of my dream
where someone said I'd be dead
in a year and it didn't phase me.
It's a spiritual journey, in
that there appears to be
a spiritual connection.
On which deck to play it?
Was so sad…
making sex promises.
Getting a little too
afterthoughtful, actual thought
where I've lost track. Where
from? Was it good?
You look good like
that, very sphinx-like. Came
with rings to spare.

A New Machine

I don't like writing much, Mike
       says.
I agree, there's times it's done
       right, but few there in that.
Song floats barbarisms.

He says, 'Poets are so horny.'
I guess it's just me.
This poem just happens to be about
       loneliness and wanting whatever
freedom the other wants,
it's the philosophers who are
       so into eros and will necessitated
by libido.
       Nihilism and narcissism recycle
the void, cooperating to undo sex
in classic service to
       static decay
but okay,
       horny, whatever.

You're keeping me honest
peeled by
a cubic wandering,
a raining paycheck, pretending
I'm Morrison. Obese, fecund,
if we share a politics, we can share…
The fumes off a needle relaying

whose hate, whose want
does incendiary speech neglect
in this lulling
        true, possibility.
I.V., I vogue, I 'ave'
committed
only to history,
plaything that was open.

It was a binary but only once;
        and not by my
        chimeric eye.
She, the long viscous mirror, shed
a tacky dress,
went about her business
        taking libations,
life spread about all intakes,
pushing through thought, drawn up
        dreaming, suppressing animal
planning, wanting animal
fucking, singing, bathing animal
        animal on animal.

Summed Up Everything

When everything is
            inverted, you appear
to dance;
the flowing up
writes a passing cloud
before heaven wrings the infinite.

You fill
            the blank that's missing,
some diversion to make me
forget what it was that I
            came here for,
trying to subvert the anti-plot to
            say something true.

Still well that is a diversion of echo,

How deep the well? How far to take
            me? — is the sobriquet
in subject conquering every cheap
            stand-in.

Have Nothing, Seek Nothing, Realize... Nothing?

EP goes to the underworld
and does not fail to bring a
spirit back with him, a
latchkey companion whose
anxious speech has been so
many years in solitude that the
book is closed, must stay
quiet to him, whose vigilant
"so that":

      - was walking around
            Chinatown backstreets
      - was reading Dr. Sax
      - was competitive with J
      - was like a ghost observing a
            dinner party

We'll see, "so that":
a multiplex was playing a Batman
      double feature,
a modern art exhibit was in the
      basement.
All ramps, no stairs.
I go off on a theory punk who's been
      into me, been
      loosely courting.
I flip through photos of him and his friends
in a pile and falling through

a revolving door,
object oriented comedy.
He comes up behind me and
tells me about his research;
I laugh and tell him he should
        "research me."

Then I am dreaming of the
Sieburth Cantos, and it
seems like a script of
        love; I flip
to the notes section.

Tolerance does not experience
        pain really.
It dozes, endures. It does not
        triumph. It does nothing.
It does not understand, it
        does not accept,
it does not burn, it does not stand,
it is an unlit stage, a
        dark auditorium, a
heaviness with hardened mouth,
anticipating the first minor
        silence "so
everlasting that":
        the obdurate beat fattens.

Grand Illusions

That I will walk there
the walk will feel like
            one second, my mind will
            be so free
that I will be alone and
            scan the fob
I will take the stairs, as I do
            when I am alone
that I will enter
and lay on the bed
and call you and ask you to
            guess where I am
that I will look through your
            books, pills, provisions
that I will be a ghost.

Apology to Mars

Is there always something
in the key of life
or a style about
the blood
as a song
of futility
a delineation
of want
to a song
of doom
of spite
of sorrow
stupid question
an apology
of horror
of unavoidable zero
in reference to all these things
to do without them
as the elegy
in our thoughts
its subject worked
all night
to lose a rhetorical slur
to find a writing
a subsequent power to view
this stand-in for some
rust colored work shirt
black Lees

black holes
brown work boots
coated in red dust
life is the transition
between showtimes
on the stair
summer's necessary nectar
from the mezzanine window
to street life cinema
subtitle track below
transmuted every night
for now
the dandelion tumbles in
original doubt
to the day's adversary
night contra light
dispossessed
the kill cult is
electric
to make me laugh
as I am laughing
language on demand
voice dictation
finger to the lips on
what I wanted
in a blue recession
bends the starlight
of the tiger in space
as with our physics
not just in space

as I am also open
burst into flames
to tell the other animals
they can rest here
where nothing
can be wrong.

Moving Day

Slowly the milestone sun
        closed,
burning, blazing sleep.

An alleyway escapes light,
someone yawned adjacent to
warm hands, belly and penis,
leans one-handed against the
        wall.

And returns to the fold,
sun blue, moving away,
taps on the glass, eyes
        speak with their eyes
tired starlings.

Afflictive and Natural Opportunities for Development

I come across some footage.
I am burning a red copy of Heidegger's
      selected.
Vengeful, he has broken my heart,
brilliant but ugly,
ugly for a monster.
Dross,
acts of faith requiring law.
Wormwood, white rose, strawberry, violet,
      watercress, primrose, heartsease,
      balm, pansy, lemon-thyme,
diamond, white quartz, white spar
      marble.
Dazzling white, snow in sun,
silence.
Expiation beware —
Marguerite & Faust, studiousness,
nothing but reptiles, you
      know me,
video of books burning, I search
      each in mind,
scanning against
orbital totalities,
and shame,
and like my idea,
we're all going to.

Pass Over the Void

Your ascetic side yields
          on the dream pike.
Your head is shaved, and I
          love you in a sexless way.
You show me a wall calendar
          from 2002
on which you've written the
albums you've listened to
          each day.
Some squares are blank;
the *Magical Mystery Tour* is
          written many times.
And that is exactly what I want
          to listen to now.
That is why you say it is no
          accident to meet here,
and that you loved me when
          and how
just a little space between us,
briefly in a life, more so in dying,
leaves a door always open,
          mouth agape,
breath, windshield glass,
something to remember
          this writer by.

All the Luck of a Fly on Ice Cream

What is thingly about you is what
        I can wing.
At times commodity,
at times contraband,
I assemble you about
my organs,
the chords,
I cannot be myself without
this stomach, heart, lungs, meat
        outside. I wing a
train in propeller,
bathe in heartsink,
what it does to my skin,
one, two, one, two
quiet wings.

All the Grapes Eaten

No mild effort on the howling
        wind's part,
'You know damn well'
on the anvil, the name
        pounding out syllabic beauties,
if you tell me which Camus you're
        working on,
I'll send you the chapter and the reference,
I have a great little book on Camus
        titled, "How the Nobel Kills."

I would be a little
        pissed and cynical, perhaps,
but I've known what I'm missing.
Unlike this path, where the
        branching sucks, and
the leaves are little yellow laughs,
a crowd's laughter that I
        shuffle through,
paint peeling from its
        corral, painted eggs,
teardrop trees,
an edgy sky where no one's walking.

Horizon cut so clean,
        where plans were drawn.
Some of those branches were abnormally long,
vining through electric wire,

power lines crossing every which way,
power and trees performing this unsubtle
      tableau.

I would agree to a tomb if it were
a book rotting
      in the middle of the library,
rest my dust,
which feels good and
should be done for
      persistent green
by the time good gets here.
      A slow cooling, we share
another helper, a further branching,
what stardom,
I, dear bright.

Put a gleaming knife
      to the midnight throat,
slayed the last silence,
touched its whimper
laid my prick
laid my knife down
bare across my species.

Injurious Plentitude

I put bowls of sugar
around the house to keep
       them from the books.

The extent we go to
       protect the things we love,
and yet do not darn socks.

We are selective machines.
We are all like CA's
       parents,
always attending
       the future and
neglecting the present.

Enlightenment needs faith,
either us or human
patronage, they alone
       return to order
to destroy it; tickles me.

Poems on films are touching
new material, visual touching
       to describe whatever
gets us off — that's my thought
       on the universe.

Time and the beautiful are constants,
they run in parallel.
That's what we call time travel,
      when we beam our brains into the
            future and
      take a leak.

Either one of us
chance smuggling,
      so that the gaps laugh
lapping, belonging together,
processional waves overlap,

      settle,
and even skeptical in this,
      return to their myth
in order to destroy it
for our structure
in love
      the alcove clone.

Light falls crashing and
kills you caressingly,
      a poured
cement, a wet
      worker-mixed
delinquency to-be, who
draws in me tonight
      this credo:
Because I poor myself
until I pour myself again.

Offshore Ondine

Surrounded by the encyclopedic asp
something is very close, one.

The main problem is promethean
always performing it
so clear-eyed through the atmospherics.

Shaken by the new language, no
        breakfast
laughing at you in your sleep
no, it's just your eyes closed
newly cleaned and ready
       to be devoured
pressing into the shore of her.

Lemon My Seaweed

The saga is tedious
the nude, stumbles
fondles flowers
is fucking the dream machine
is barely morning 3:30am
bright, blaring condition
pants, and you eat
party, and you consider sleep
vodka aiding
a bruised groin
the tender twenties
and wants love to grow like
       the belly, digestive.

Ethics of Ambiguity

Continuing my exploration
of what reproducibility
means as the self-same
      force, that's
one approach
to decomposition, in itself
is a concept wedged between
time and history – an 'and'
to repeat after every
step, and the step unchanging.

The opposite of glaciers
      above us,
the clouds move and here
      we stand still,
rough edges, that 'bad'
or really 'softer' more
      silk than scarring
diminutive, I don't
      understand
smaller and smaller
      possessions,
conversations performed
deeper, closer
to a single point
from which are paid
      leaves.
Seen exhibiting abnormal

behavior on the night of
September 15,
abandon yourself and your
inhibitions, would this not
be better
than the cud that never downs
but says all
flesh is essentially the
same movement from
matter to creature, but
I've heard it tastes different.

The punctum can listen without
knowing how, like a child
was even listening. There is
the bare stage strangeness
very anti-radio, anti-savior,
and then you perform
radio-theater, which is
presented on bare action.

With No Song

I break for hours,
we make love on the sofa,
it's a boat,
then I want to write again.

And when my muse is sad, so am I.
I write a death poem
with no song.

I read the books of my peers
and close my window because
       the couple downstairs
       is using a table saw, it
       ricochets down the townhouse
blank faces, will they never stop?

It is Saturday,
I want to write again,
we make love,
when my muse is sad, I am lost.
It is like the ocean being lost
       in a day.

Impossibility is spread on toast,
       simple signature,
the drilling does not stop.
It's not an infinite well, it's simple.

Radiant Heat

I read the intro to
the Hackett Publishing Co.'s
Complete Works of Plato,
take the information there very
        seriously as I am reading it.
Aside from
suggesting that the concept of an
early, middle and late period
is tenuous if not fabricated, it
states that all we know
        of this wrestler's
bibliography is traced to
a single thinker. The editor
makes a case for the dialogous
in the dialogs, saying we need
        to express and
re-express the subjects sounded
there through our own circumstance.
It's funny that way.
It's becoming less and less interesting,
what the ancients did.
Styled colloquial
with no suppositions, all the
        alternatives spread
like a table of winning
        hands in retrospect.
One caster off the red velvet
ottoman, you falling

towards that pond for eyes,
        night swimming.
What the hag
        does with them
when she collects
yesterday's prayers over
flame retardant tears
after sleeping
in white wax, says there's no
baptism, no how
        to say the names.
One by one
group suicide by the flies,
the quartet
        kicks it
in all types of December, and this
        opportunity for species
cooling, changing,
        never mind my other
        indiscretions
in the morning's blackest hour.
I sprung up from a mild peace,
illustrious, though useless.
Play dead, no, we cannot
        stay dismissive for daybreak,
tired eyes rubbing,
stay there.
No one says, 'the bath is too hot,'
but it is, and that's why I'm sitting
on the floor

the towels
are things
that were
this rose bottom,
or a plane ever holding
        not just anything
        that buzzed
between planks
born in walls.
Applying a selective desire takes stamina.
Every stone is present, the physical aspect
        of what will be done.
We will read, and yes, collect materials
        to burn
        as a cruel joke.
The ancients also competed among failed works.
This friend called life still having me.

Disabused Migrations

Perhaps I do have other things on my mind,

       — to get by
       — by way of pool
       — cheap players
       — friendships made to last that lack those
things she thought were
         supposed to improve a real happiness, in
the sense of life's
       meaning.

Perhaps I do dream poorly.

And sounds can frighten me, that I am animal.

Perhaps I shouldn't be driving.

I am distracted by the moon, moving water,
carnivals, bikers.

That I was born to the sound of bombs.

Mistrust with most persons in groups.

Severely open to strangers.

Subject: poetry, denial.

I am distracted by song, I sing.

Perhaps the present is not to be mentioned.

There is no box to check for anyone's kind mistrust.

They don't want anyone better than they are nor do canned superlatives.

That my attitude needs a job.

There needn't be a formal response to the outrage we bastards feel as bards.

As close and dark as you can.

We call this feeding hour.

I and thou, the harder they come.

ACKNOWLEDGMENTS

Excerpts from this text and versions of several poems have previously been published in the journals *Baited Area* (Vol. 6, Fall 2022), *The Poetry Project Newsletter* (Winter, 2022), *luigitenco* (Vol. 3, Summer 2023) and the chapbooks *At Crepuscule Remembering Aquaducts* (Wonder, 2024), *Protest and Orison* (Belladonna, 2024), and *Hieroglyphics Then and Now* (Spiral Editions, 2024.)

Rachelle Rahmé is a poet and scholar interested in creative liberation methodologies. Born in Lebanon, she lives in Brooklyn, NY. Rahmé is the author of several chapbooks from *72 Press*, *blush*, *Wonder*, *Belladonna Collective*, and *Spiral Editions,* as well as a speculative fiction novella from *Aventures Ltd* and a collection of translations of the occupation poetry of philosopher Georges Bataille from *o-blēk*. She holds a BFA in Film from New York University, a MA in Philosophy from The New School, and an MFA in Literary Arts from Brown University. She was a recipient of The Poetry Project's Emerge-Surface-Be Fellowship in 2021-2022.

FONO
GRAꟻ

1. **Eileen Myles**—*Aloha/irish trees* (LP)

2. **Rae Armantrout**—*Conflation* (LP)

3. **Alice Notley**—*Live in Seattle* (LP)

4. **Harmony Holiday**—*The Black Saint and the Sinnerman* (LP)

5. **Susan Howe & Nathaniel Mackey**—*STRAY: A Graphic Tone* (LP)

6. **Annelyse Gelman & Jason Grier**—*About Repulsion* (EP)

7. **Joshua Beckman**—*Some Mechanical Poems To Be Read Aloud* (print)

8. **Dao Strom**—*Instrument/ Traveler's Ode* (print; cassette tape)

9. **Douglas Kearney & Val Jeanty**—*Fodder* (LP)

10. **Mark Leidner**—*Returning the Sword to the Stone* (print)

11. **Charles Valle**—*Proof of Stake: An Elegy* (print)

12. **Emily Kendal Frey**—*LOVABILITY* (print)

13. **Brian Laidlaw and the Family Trade**—*THIS ASTER: adaptations of Emile Nelligan* (LP)

14. **Nathaniel Mackey and The Creaking Breeze Ensemble**—*Fugitive Equation* (compact disc)

15. *FE Magazine* (print)

16. **Brandi Katherine Herrera**—*MOTHER IS A BODY* (print)

17. **Jan Verberkmoes**—*Firewatch* (print)

18. **Krystal Languell**—*Systems Thinking with Flowers* (print)

19. **Matvei Yankelevich**—*Dead Winter* (print)

20. **Cody-Rose Clevidence**—*Dearth & God's Green Mirth* (print)

21. **Hilary Plum**—*Hole Studies* (print)

22. **John Ashbery**—*Live at Sanders Theatre, 1976* (LP)

23. **Alice Notley**—*The Speak Angel Series* (print)

24. **Alice Notley**—*Early Works* (print)

25. **Joshua Marie Wilkinson**—*Trouble Finds You* (print)

26. **Timmy Straw**—*The Thomas Salto* (print)

27. **Audre Lorde**—*At Fassett Studio, 1970* (LP)

28. **Gabriel Palacios**—*A Ten Peso Burial For Which Truth I Sign* (print)

29. **Isabel Zapata, trans. Robin Myers**—*A Whale Is a Country* (print)

30. **Callum Angus**—*Cataract* (print)

31. *FE/De-Canon Anthology* (print)

32. **Cody-Rose Clevidence**—*The Grimace of Eden, Now* (print)

33. **Jaydra Johnson**—*Low: Notes on Art and Trash* (print)

34. **Jaime Gil de Biedma**—*If Only For a Moment (I'll Never Be Young Again)* (print)

35. **Esther Kondo Heller**—*AR:RANGE:MENTS* (print)

36. **Ahmad Almallah**—*Wrong Winds* (print)

37. **Kimberly Alidio**—*Traceable Relation* (print)

38. **Sara Gilmore**—*The Green Lives* (print)

39. **Darcie Dennigan**—*Little Neck* (print)

40. **Nora Claire Miller**—*Groceries* (print)

Fonograf Editions is a registered 501(c)(3) nonprofit organization. Find more information about the press at: fonografeditions.com.